an ENEMY called
AVERAGE

the KEYS to unlocking your DREAMS

John Mason

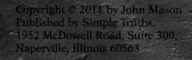

Copyright © 2011 by John Mason
Published by Simple Truths,
1952 McDowell Road, Suite 300,
Naperville, Illinois 60563

Simple Truths is a registered trademark.
Printed and bound in the United States of America.

www.simpletruths.com
Toll Free 800-900-3427
Book Design: Simple Truths, Designer : Lynn Harker

Images by: Istockphoto, ThinkStock and ShutterStock images

ISBN 978-1-60810-133-7

04 WOZ 12

DEDICATION

I am proud to dedicate this book to my beautiful wife, Linda, and our four wonderful children—Michelle, Greg, Mike, and Dave.

To Linda, for her laughter and love;

To Michelle, for her creativity and utmost professionalism;

To Greg, for his patient perseverance and free golf lessons;

To Mike, for his inventiveness and keen perception;

To Dave, for his unbridled enthusiasm and contagious smile;

Without their support, help, encouragement, sense of humor, and prayers, I would never have been able to do what I've been blessed to do.

TABLE OF CONTENTS

INTRODUCTION

M

№ 1

Your
**LEAST
FAVORITE**
color should
be **BEIGE.**

Exciting, innovative, transforming, productive … words you never associate with beige. Rather, beige brings to mind words like neutral, apathetic and dull … something no one wants a part of.

Here's a great opportunity. Choose to be a person who is on the offensive, not the defensive. Never try to defend your present position and situation. People who live defensively never rise above being average. You will find when all of your reasons are defensive your cause almost never succeeds.

Decide to be on the offensive, to take the initiative. Lukewarm, indecisive people are never secure regardless of their wealth, education or position.

Never let your quest for balance become an excuse to stay the same. Take the unique, radical, invading move you know you're supposed to take. Many times the attempt to maintain balance in life is really just an excuse to be lukewarm.

When you choose to be on the offensive, the atmosphere of your life will begin to change. It's a decision made within.

When you do choose to be on the offensive, keep all your conflicts impersonal. Fight the issue, not the person. Speak about what you can do, not what others are incapable of doing.

Being on the offensive and taking the initiative are master keys that open doors of opportunity in your life. Learn to create a habit of taking the initiative and ***don't ever start your day in neutral.*** Every morning when your feet hit the floor, you should be thinking on the offensive, moving forward, taking control of your day and your life.

Pulling back and being defensive usually enhances the problem. Intimidation always precedes defeat.

Be like the two fishermen who got trapped in a storm in the middle of a lake. One turned to the other and asked, "Should we plan, or should we row?" His wise companion responded, "Let's do both!"

That's taking the offensive.

№ 2

"The NOSE of **THE BULLDOG** is slanted backwards so he can continue to breathe **WITHOUT LETTING GO.**"

~ Winston Churchill ~

Persistent people begin their success where most others quit. Here's a simple key to success in any area of your life; be known as a person of persistence and endurance. One person with commitment, persistence and endurance will accomplish more than a thousand people with interest alone. The more diligently we work, the harder it is to quit. **Persistence is a habit—so is quitting.**

Never worry about how much money, ability or equipment you are starting with; just begin with a million dollars' worth of determination. Remember: It's not what you have, it's what you do with what you have that makes all the difference. Many people eagerly begin "the race to the dream," but they forget to add patience, persistence and endurance to their enthusiasm. Josh Billings said, "Consider the postage stamp. Its usefulness consists in the ability to stick to one thing until it gets there." We can learn a lot from that little ol' stamp.

The choice of giving up or going on is a defining moment in your life.

There were two men shipwrecked on this island. The minute they got onto the island one of them started screaming and yelling, "We're going to die! We're going to die! There's no food! No water! We're going to die!"

The second man was propped up against a palm tree and

acting so calmly it drove the first man crazy.

"Don't you understand? We're going to die!!"

The second man replied, "You don't understand, I make $100,000 a week."

The first man looked at him quite dumbfounded and asked, "What difference does that make?

We're on an island with no food and no water! We're going to die!!!"

The second man answered, "You just don't get it. I make $100,000 a week and I tithe ten percent on that $100,000 a week. My pastor will find me!"

When you're persistent, you know it and so does everyone else.

Many times our dreams and plans appear not to be succeeding. We are tempted to give up and quit trying. Instead, we need to continue to water and fertilize those dreams, nurturing the seeds of the vision within us. Knowing if we do not quit, if we display perseverance and endurance, we will eventually win. Charles Haddon Spurgeon said, "By perseverance the snail reached the ark." We need to be like that snail … and postage stamp … and bulldog.

Here's my challenge to you today. Become famous for completing important, challenging tasks.

I promise
you this ...
you will be
shocked at the
IMPACT of your
PERSISTENCE.

Nº 3

SMILE.

It ADDS to your face VALUE.

What would happen if you were the happiest, most enthusiastic person you know? Would it shock everyone in your world? Would it change the way people felt about you?

Smiling—being happy and enthusiastic—is always a choice, not a result. It's a decision that must be consciously made. Enthusiasm, joy and happiness will improve your personality and people's opinion of you. It will help you keep a proper perspective on life. Helen Keller said, "Keep your face to the sunshine, and you cannot see the shadow."

The bigger the challenge you are facing, the more enthusiasm you need. Our attitude always tells others what we expect in return.

A smile is a powerful weapon. It can break the ice in tough situations. You will find being enthusiastic is like having a head cold; both are very contagious. A laugh a day will keep negative people away. As enthusiasm increases, stress and fear will decrease.

Many people say, "Well, no wonder those people are happy, confident, and positive; if I had their job and assets, I would be happy too!" Such false thinking assumes successful people are positive because they have a good income and lots of possessions. But the reverse is true. Such people probably have a good income and lots of possessions as a result of being positive, confident and happy.

Enthusiasm always inspires action. No significant accomplishment has ever been made without it. You can succeed at almost anything when you have limitless enthusiasm. It moves the world.

Your enthusiasm reflects your reserves, your unexploited resources and perhaps your future because it isn't our position, but our disposition that makes us happy. Remember, some people freeze in the winter. Others ski. **A positive attitude always creates positive results.** There is a direct correlation between our passion and our potential. Attitude is a little thing that makes a big difference. Depression, gloom, pessimism, despair, discouragement and fear slay more human beings than all illnesses combined.

I agree with Winston Churchill when he said, "I am an optimist. It does not seem too much use being anything else."

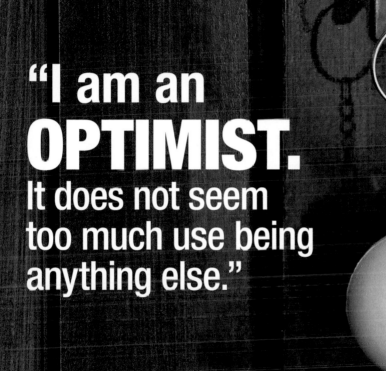

"I am an **OPTIMIST.** It does not seem too much use being anything else."

N⁰. 4

Those who don't take CHANCES don't make ADVANCES.

All the great discoveries have been made by people with great vision. Significant achievements have never been obtained by taking small risks on unimportant issues. Do not waste time planning, analyzing and risking on small ideas. It is always wise to spend more time on decisions that are irreversible and less on those that are reversible.

Learn to stretch and reach way out. **Aim high and take risks.** Average people only look to next year based on last year. Instead, reach for the potential; don't just plan based on the past. How can you drive where you want to go, if you're looking in the rear view mirror?

Those who make great strides take chances and plan past the challenges of life. Go out on a limb ... that's where the fruit is.

Almost nothing in life is more frustrating than becoming really good at unimportant tasks. Don't become so caught up in the small matters you cannot take advantage of important opportunities. Most people spend their entire lives lowering buckets into empty wells and then waste their days trying to pull them up again and again.

Choose to dream big; strive to reach the full potential of your life.

Choose to focus on the important issues of life, not the unimportant. H. Stern said, "If you're hunting rabbits in tiger country, you must keep your eye peeled for tigers, but when you are hunting tigers, you can ignore the rabbits." There are plenty of tigers to go around. Do not be distracted by the rabbits of life. Set your sights on bigger game.

Security and opportunity are total strangers. If an undertaking does not include risk, it is not worthy of being called a real dream.

A famous old saying goes like this, ***"Even a turtle doesn't get ahead unless he sticks his neck out."*** Dream big! There's no other way to ***really*** live.

Dream
BIG!

N°: 5

Never surrender
YOUR DREAM
to noisy
negatives.

Nobody can ever make you feel average without your permission. Ingratitude and criticism are going to come; they are part of the price you pay for leaping past mediocrity. Instead of being surprised by ingratitude, we should expect it.

If you have success, you will be criticized. The only way to avoid criticism is to do nothing and be nothing. Those who do things inevitably stir-up criticism. Remember sticks and stones are only thrown at fruit bearing trees.

Have you ever noticed those who don't succeed are always the first to tell you how? No one can get ahead of you by kicking you in the seat of the pants. Those who are throwing mud are simultaneously losing ground. A successful person is one who can lay a firm foundation with the bricks others throw at him.

My feeling is the person who says it cannot be done should not interrupt the one who is doing it. Kenneth Tynan provided the best description of a critic I have ever heard. "A critic," he said, "Is a man who knows the way but can't drive the car."

Most of the time, people who are critical are either jealous or uninformed. They usually say things that have no impact whatsoever on truth. There's a famous quote by William R. Inge that describes this situation perfectly: ***"It is useless for the sheep to pass resolutions in favor of vegetarianism while the wolf remains of a different opinion."***

The fact is when you make your mark in life, you'll always attract erasers. The first and great commandment about critics is: **Don't let them scare you.** Charles Dodgson said, "If you limit your actions in life to things that nobody could possibly find fault with, you will not do much."

Nothing significant has ever been accomplished without controversy, without criticism. When you allow other people's words to stop you, they will. How you choose to respond to criticism is one of the most important decisions you make.

Remember this: If you are afraid of criticism, you will die doing nothing. If you want a place in the sun, you will have to expect some blisters and some sand kicked in your face. Criticism is a compliment when you know what you're doing is right.

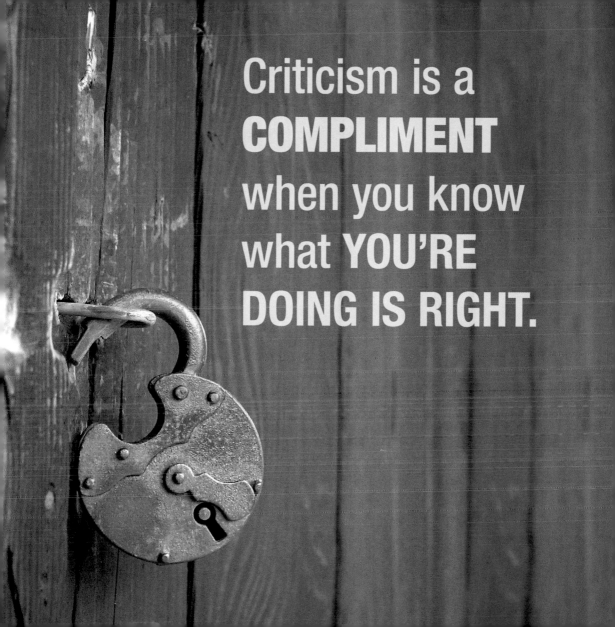

Criticism is a **COMPLIMENT** when you know what **YOU'RE DOING IS RIGHT.**

Nº 6

Your **BEST FRIENDS** are those who bring out the **BEST IN YOU.**

Misery wants your company, but you don't have to join in.

A number of years ago I found myself at a stagnation point in my life. I was unproductive and indecisive about the right direction for my life. One day I noticed almost all of my friends were in the same situation. When we got together, our problems were all we talked about. As I considered this predicament, it became clear to me I needed better relationships. I needed what I call "foundational-level" people in my life. Such people bring out the best in us and influence us to become better people. They cause us to have greater vision and confidence and to see things from the right perspective.

Without hesitation, I radically changed my closest associations. Not surprisingly my life changed … for the better. It was a defining moment in my life.

I have found it is better to be alone than in the wrong company. A single conversation with the right person can be more valuable than years of study. Whoever doesn't increase you, will eventually decrease you.

Steer clear of negative-thinking "experts." Remember: In the eyes of average people, average is always considered outstanding.

Tell me who your friends are, and I will tell you who you are. The **less** you associate with some people, the **more** your life will improve. If you run with wolves you will learn how to howl. But, if you associate with eagles, you will learn how to soar.

If you were to list your greatest benefits, resources or strengths, you would find that money is one of the least important ones while some of your greatest resources are the people you know. My friend, Mike Murdock said, "Someone is always observing you who is capable of greatly blessing you."

Look carefully at the closest associations in your life; it's an indication of the direction you're heading.

If you associate
with **EAGLES**,
you will learn
how to **SOAR**.

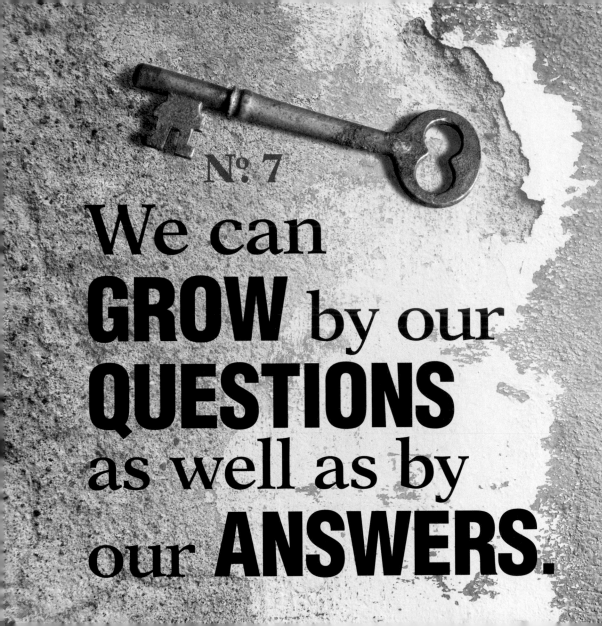

№ 7

We can **GROW** by our **QUESTIONS** as well as by our **ANSWERS.**

Here are some IMPORTANT QUESTIONS we should ask ourselves:

1. What one decision would I make if I knew it would not fail?

2. How old is my attitude?

3. In what areas do I claim faith, but my actions say unbelief?

4. If everyone in the United States of America were at my level of commitment, would there be prosperity in the land?

5. Do my competitors know who I am?

6. Am I running from something, or to something?

7. What can I do to make better use of my time?

8. Would the boy/girl I was be proud of the man/woman I am?

9. What one thing should I eliminate from my life because it holds me back from reaching my full potential?

10. Has failure gone to my head?

11. What impossible thing am I believing and planning for?

12. What is my most prevailing thought?

13. What good thing that I committed to do have I quit doing?

14. How have the people I respect earned that respect?

15. What would a truly creative person do in my situation?

16. What outside influences are causing me to be better or worse?

17. Where are my daily habits taking me?

18. What gifts, talents or strengths do I have?

19. What is one thing I can do for someone else who has no opportunity to repay me?

Life's most IMPORTANT ANSWERS are found in asking the right questions.

How
much
have
you
grown?

N⁰ 8

A man with ONE watch knows **WHAT TIME IT** is; a man with TWO watches is **NEVER QUITE SURE.**

~ Lee Segall ~

Think about it. Aren't some of the most miserable, unhappy people you know ones who can never make a decision? When the mind is in doubt, it's easily swayed by slight impulses, opening the door to many wrong decisions. Indecision causes things to go from bad to worse. The middle of the road is a dangerous place to be and the worst place to try and go forward.

Choose to be the most decisive person you know. Have a will, not just a wish. An indecisive person allows instability to creep into every area of life. If you don't decide what is important, you will spend your life doing only what is important to others.

A greater degree of wishful thinking leads to a greater degree of mediocrity. Being decisive, being focused, and committing ourselves to the fulfillment of a dream greatly increases our probability of success and at the same time closes the door to wrong options.

The challenge is to be decisive dreamers. Harry Truman once said, "Some questions cannot be answered, but they can be decided." Even when we don't have all the facts available, we usually have all the facts needed to make a decision.

Don't be afraid to make a choice. We should make decisions, even if it means we'll sometimes be wrong. If you hear yourself saying,

"I've decided," you're on the path to a successful, productive life.

Choice, not chance, determines destiny. Too many people go through life not knowing what they want, but feeling sure they don't have it. Herbert Prochnow said, "There is a time when we must firmly choose the course which we will follow, or the endless drift of events will make the decision for us."

Too many people are like wheelbarrows, trailers or canoes. They need to be pushed, pulled or paddled. You're either moving other people to decisions or they're moving you. Decide to do something now to make your life better. The choice is yours.

Bertrand Russell said, "Nothing is so exhausting as indecision, and nothing is so futile."

Your destiny is not a matter of chance; it's a matter of choice. Many people have the right aims in life; they just never get around to pulling the trigger.

Indecisive people are like a blind man looking in a dark room for a black cat that isn't there. The fact is that decisive people typically prevail because everybody else is so indecisive.

N⁰ 9

The **BEST**
time of day
is **NOW.**

Procrastination is a killer.

When you kill time, you kill the purpose and dreams within you. A wise old saying says, "If you wait for perfect conditions, you'll never get anything done."

The first step to overcoming procrastination is to eliminate all excuses for not taking immediate action.

The second step is to not be so busy! Everyone is always on the move. People are moving forwards, backwards, and sometimes nowhere at all as though they are on a treadmill. The mistake most people make is thinking the main goal of life is to stay busy. Such thinking is a trap. What is important is not whether you are busy, but whether you are progressing. The question is one of activity versus accomplishment.

41

A gentleman named Jean Henri Fabre conducted an experiment with processionary caterpillars. They are so named because they have a habit of blindly following each other no matter how they are lined up or where they are going. In his experiment, Fabre placed these tiny creatures in a circle. For 24 hours, the caterpillars dutifully followed one another around and around and around. Then Fabre placed the caterpillars around a saucer full of pine needles (their favorite food). For six days, the mindless creatures moved around and around the saucer, dying from starvation and exhaustion even though an abundance of choice food was located less than two inches away.

The caterpillars were very active, but they were not accomplishing anything. They had confused activity with accomplishment.

Be known as someone who accomplishes things—not one who simply talks about it. Have you noticed, procrastinators are good at talking, not doing? Mark Twain said, "Noise proves nothing. Often a hen who has merely laid an egg cackles as if she laid an asteroid."

Occasionally you may see someone who doesn't do anything yet seems to be successful in life. Don't be deceived. Remember the old saying, "Even a broken clock is right twice a day." Make progress—not excuses.

I have found this to be true: The longer we take to act on an idea, the more unclear it becomes. Procrastination is a choice that holds us back and makes us miss the best opportunities.

Procrastination is a choice that *holds us back* and makes us *miss* *the best* **OPPORTUNITIES.**

Nº 10

FEAR and **WORRY** are interest paid in advance on something you **MAY NEVER OWN.**

Would you pay interest in advance on a car you know you'd never drive? Or a house you know you'd never move into? Of course you wouldn't. But isn't that the way fear tries to operate in our lives?

Fear is a poor chisel for carving out tomorrow. Today, if you're viewing your future from a position of fear, that view is wrong. Psychologists tell us nearly everything we worry about, doesn't happen.

Worry is simply allowing fear to triumph over what you believe.

A woman was crying profusely and standing on a street corner. A man came up to her and asked why she was weeping. The lady shook her head and replied: "I was just thinking maybe someday I would get married. We would later have a beautiful baby girl. Then one day this child and I would go for a walk along this street, and my darling daughter would run into the street, get hit by a car, and die."

It sounds like a pretty ridiculous situation—weeping because of something that will probably never happen. Yet we act this way when we worry. We blow a situation out of proportion that might never come to pass. And here's the biggest danger, fear causes us not to attempt where we should have dared to go.

An old Swedish proverb says, "Worry gives a small thing a big shadow." Worry is simply the misuse of the creative imagination within each of us. When fear rises in our mind, we should learn to expect the opposite in our lives. The opposite of fear is belief of a positive future.

The word *worry* is derived from an Anglo-Saxon term meaning to *strangle* or to *choke off.* There is no question worry and fears choke off everything positive and productive in our lives.

Things are seldom as they seem. "Skim milk masquerades as cream," said W.S. Gilbert. As we dwell on and worry about matters beyond our control, a negative effect begins to set in. Too much analysis always leads to paralysis. Worry is a route that leads from somewhere to nowhere. Never let it direct your life.

No. 11

Our **WORDS** are seeds planted in other **PEOPLE'S LIVES.**

What we say is important. Our vocabulary should be filled with words of hope and dreams. Be known as someone who speaks positively.

Recently I saw a sign under a mounted large mouth bass. It read, "If I had kept my mouth shut I wouldn't be here." How true! Don't jump into trouble mouth first.

Let me pose this question to you: Starting today what would happen if you changed what you said about your biggest problem, your biggest opportunity?

I don't know if you've had this conversation or not, but last month I turned to my wife, Linda, while we were sitting together in our family room and said, "Just so you know, I never want to live in a vegetative state dependent on some machine. If that ever happens, just pull the plug."

She immediately got up, walked over and unplugged the TV.

"Our words create our worlds," says Dean Sikes. Your words have the power to start fires or quench passion.

Don't be like the man who joined a monastery in which the monks were allowed to speak only two words every seven years. After the first seven years had passed, the new initiate met with the abbot, who asked him, "Well, what are your two words?"

"Food's bad," replied the man, who then went back to his silence.

Seven years later the clergyman asked, "What are your two words now?"

"Bed's hard," the man responded.

Seven years later—twenty-one years after his initial entry into the monastery—the man met with the abbot for the third and final time. "And what are your two words this time?" the abbot asked.

"I quit."

"Well, I'm not surprised," the cleric answered disgustedly. "All you've done since you got here is complain!"

Don't be like that man; don't be known as a person whose only words are negative. If you're a member of the "negative grapevine," resign.

Contrary to what you may have heard, talk is not cheap.

Nº 12

⁵²

A **GOAL** is a dream with a **DEADLINE.**

Your vision must be written. When you keep a vision in your mind, it is not really a goal; it is nothing more than a dream. There is power in putting that dream on paper. When you commit something to writing, commitment to achievement naturally follows.

Another key is to take action and run with the vision in your life. As long as you are running with the vision, you will not turn around. When you walk with a vision, it's easy to change directions and go the wrong way. You cannot stroll to a goal.

I read this recently, "Any enterprise is built by wise planning, becomes strong through common sense, and profits wonderfully by keeping abreast of the facts." Simply stated, effective goal-setting provides an opportunity to bring the future to the present so you can deal with it today. You will find achievement is easy when your outer goals become inner commitment.

We all need to prepare. The first choice for us in any situation can't be disorder or to waste funds. That's why proper planning is so important. When you plan, plan for potential. Believe your biggest dream. When you plan, look to the future, not to the past. You cannot drive forward effectively when you are looking out the rear window.

Look outside yourself because that's where the biggest opportunities are found. At the beginning, every great success seems impossible.

We all have opportunity for success. Having a bad life requires as much energy as having a good life, yet most people live meaningless lives because they never decide to write their vision down and then follow through. If you cannot see the goal, you cannot go toward it.

Here's an unseen bonus with this type of action: What you learn on the path to your goals is actually more valuable than achieving the goal itself. Columbus discovered America while searching for a route to India. Be on the lookout for the "Americas" in your path. Put the vision for your life on paper and begin to run full speed ahead towards it.

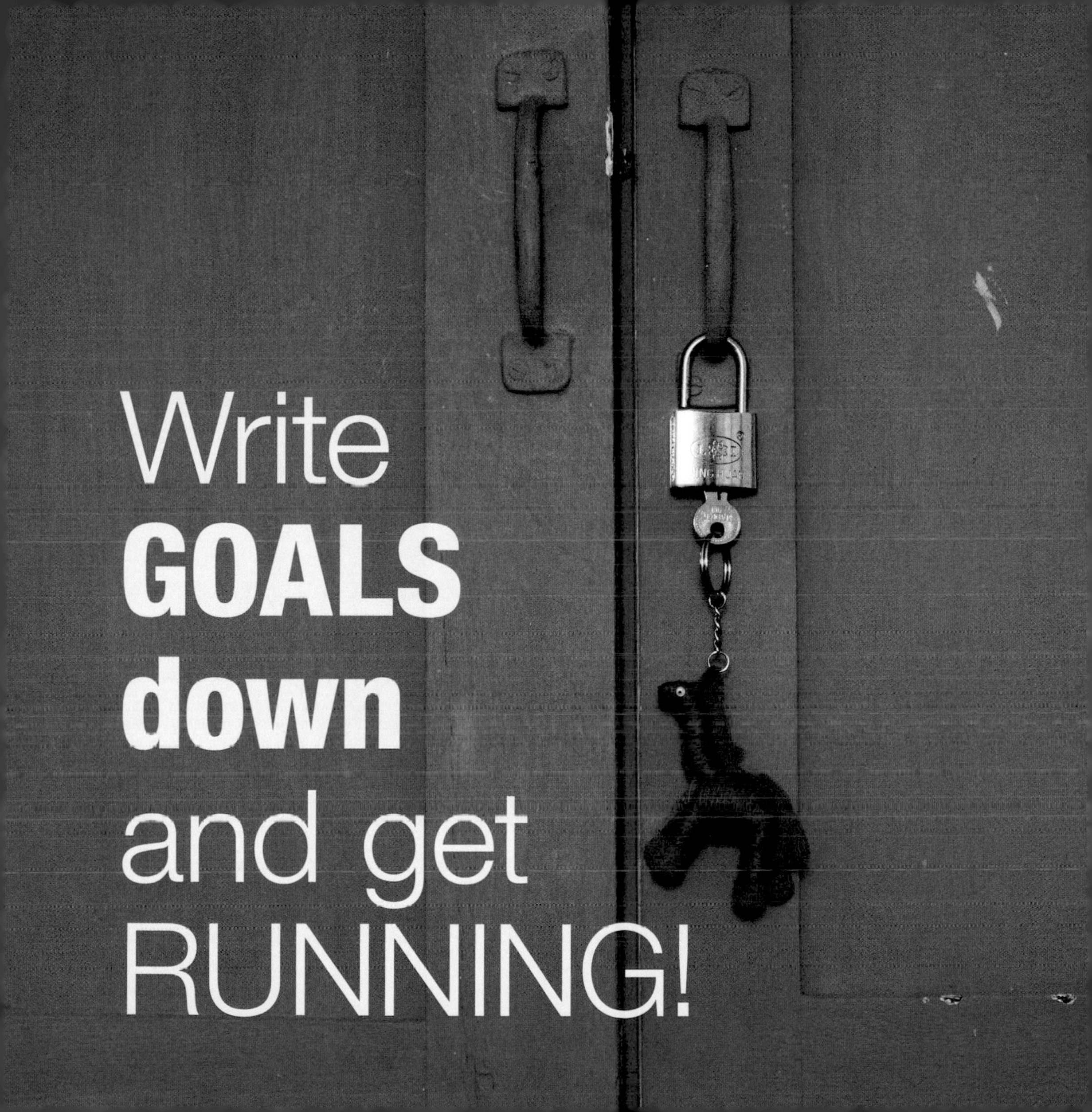
Write
GOALS
down
and get
RUNNING!

Nº. 13

The most natural **THING TO DO** when you get knocked down is **GET BACK UP.**

56

How you respond to failures and mistakes is one of the most important decisions you make every day.

We all experience failures and make mistakes. In fact, successful people always have more failure in their lives than average people do.

Those who don't expect anything are never disappointed; those who never try, never fail. Anyone who is currently achieving anything in life is simultaneously risking failure. It is always better to fail in doing something than to excel at doing nothing. I like to put it this way, "A flawed diamond is more valuable than a perfect brick." People who have no failures also have few victories.

Everybody gets knocked down. It is how fast they get up that counts. There is a positive correlation between a success mentality and how quickly a person responds to failures and mistakes. The greater degree of success mentality, the greater the capacity to get up and go on. The less success mentality, the longer people hold onto past failures. Instead of seeing yourself as a failure, see yourself as a learner.

We truly fail only when we do not learn from an experience. The decision is up to us. We can choose to turn a failure into a hitching post or a guidepost in our lives. ***There is always the opportunity***

to learn from failure.

Here is the key to being free from the stranglehold of past failures and mistakes: *Learn the lesson and forget the details.* Gain from the experience, but do not roll the minute details of it over and over in your mind. Build on the experience, and get on with your life. When you fall, bounce as high as you can!

> *Perseverance* is
> failing 19 times and
> *succeeding the 20th.*
>
> JULIE ANDREWS

When
you fall,
BOUNCE
as **HIGH**
as you
CAN!

Nº 14

GROWTH comes more from BUILDING on TALENTS, GIFTS, and STRENGTHS— than by solving problems.

I'd like to ask you an important question: Are you trying to be someone you're not? You may feel like you've given up on being you or that you can never be what you once thought you could. I believe there's something deep inside every person that says, "I've been created a certain unique way … on purpose for a purpose."

Too many people ignore the gifts and talents within them. It is amazing how some people can devote their entire life to a field of endeavor or a profession that has nothing to do with their inborn talents. In fact, many people spend their lifetime trying to change who they really are. They ignore their personal composition while constantly seeking to change their natural makeup. Instead, each of us should recognize our innate gifts, talents and strengths and do everything in our power to build on them.

Your talents and strengths are permanent and enduring. Even if you've never done anything with them, even if you've failed time and time again, those gifts and strengths still reside within you. They are there this very day. Take this powerful step. Simply choose to do something with them, beginning right now.

Gifts and talents are deposits in our personal accounts, but we determine the interest on them. The greater the amount of interest and attention we give to them, the greater their value becomes. Because they're not loans, they are never used up or depleted. In fact, the more we use them, the greater, stronger and more valuable they become. When we put them to good use, they provide information, insight and results that cannot be accomplished in any other way or from any other source. ***The fact is, every person has been given the ability to do certain things well.***

Each of us should make full use of ***all*** of our gifts and talents so we don't abound in one area while becoming bankrupt in all the others. There's a quote by Abraham Maslow, "If the only tool you have is a hammer, you tend to see every problem as a nail." Don't make that mistake; use all of the gifts you have.

Never underestimate the purpose of the gifts within you. They are given to us not only to fulfill the purpose in our own lives, but also so we can help others. There are people whose lives are waiting to be affected by what's within you. So evaluate yourself. ***Define and refine your gifts, talents and strengths.***

Choose **TODAY** to take on **OPPORTUNITIES** to exercise your unique talents and watch *growth surround you.*

N°: 15

None of the
secrets of
SUCCESS will
work unless
YOU DO.

Rising above mediocrity never just happens; it is always a result of a dream combined with work. Vision without action is like gold within the earth. It is of no value until it is mined out.

Success principles multiplied by nothing equal nothing.

Put your dream into action. Do not wait for your ship to come in; swim to it! Thomas Edison said it best, "Opportunity is missed by most people because it is dressed in overalls and looks like work." True vision has hands and feet; it takes action. It is not enough to **know that you know.** *It is more important to **show** that you know.*

When true belief and hard work operate together, the result is a masterpiece. George Bernard Shaw said, "When I was young, I observed that nine out of every ten things I did were failures. So I did ten times more work."

The founder of Holiday Inn, Kemmons Wilson, replied to those who asked him how he became successful by saying, "I really don't know why I'm here. I never got a degree, and I've only worked half days my entire life. I guess my advice is to do the same, work half days every day. And it doesn't matter which half … the first twelve hours or the second twelve hours."

You can't fulfill your destiny on a theory ... it takes **WORK**. Success simply takes good ideas and puts them into action. What the *free enterprise* system really means is that the more *enterprising* you are the more *free* you are. What this country needs is less emphasis on *free* and more on *enterprise*.

"Striving for success without hard work is like trying to harvest where you haven't planted," said David Bly. What you believe doesn't amount to very much unless it causes you to climb out of the grandstand and onto the playing field. You cannot just dream yourself into what you could be.

Some say *nothing* is impossible, yet there are a lot of people doing *nothing* every day. Tap into the power that is produced when a dream is mixed with action and then watch something amazing happen.

You can't fulfill your DESTINY
on a theory ...

It takes
WORK.

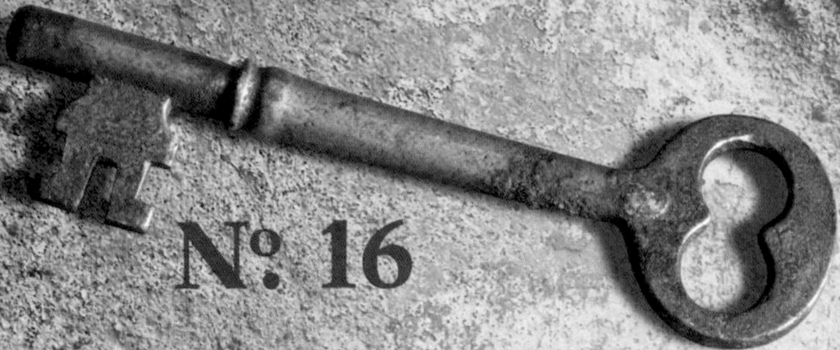

№ 16

Option one VERSUS Option two

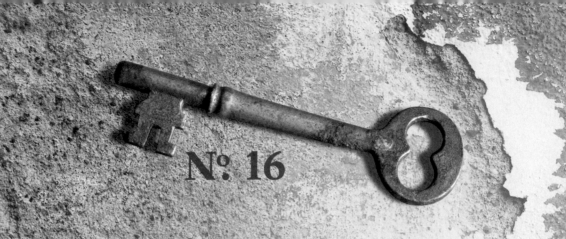

We make decisions every day. We're confronted daily with options. We must choose one or the other.

Being better **VERSUS** being bitter

Decisiveness **VERSUS** indifference

Enthusiasm **VERSUS** being lukewarm

"How we can" **VERSUS** "if we can" statements

Saying "get up" **VERSUS** saying "give up"

Security **VERSUS** risk

Overcoming problems **VERSUS** coping with problems

Standing out **VERSUS** blending in

Steering **VERSUS** drifting

How much we get done **VERSUS** how much we attempt to do

Opposing dishonesty **VERSUS** coexisting with dishonesty

Development **VERSUS** destruction

Obtaining **VERSUS** complaining

Committing **VERSUS** trying

Peace **VERSUS** strife

Choice **VERSUS** chance

Determination **VERSUS** discouragement

Growing **VERSUS** dying

Demanding more of ourselves **VERSUS** excusing ourselves

Doing for others **VERSUS** doing for ourselves

Progressing **VERSUS** regressing

Priorities **VERSUS** aimlessness

Accountability **VERSUS** irresponsibility

Action **VERSUS** activity

Solutions **VERSUS** problems

More of good **VERSUS** more of everything else

Being in *Who's Who* **VERSUS** asking "Why me?"

Nº 17

Being a SERVANT won't make you famous, JUST RICH.

There is always room at the top for anyone who is willing to say, "I'll serve," and means it.

Several years ago I was listening to Zig Ziglar. In his presentation he said, "You'll always have everything in life you want if you'll help enough other people get what they want." When I heard that statement, something went off inside of me. I made a conscious decision to incorporate that concept into my life. It has made a tremendous difference.

True leadership always begins with servanthood. We should serve those whom we lead. Be willing to serve without trying to reap the benefits. Before looking for a way to get, look for a way to give. Even postage stamps become useless when they get stuck on themselves.

If you are only looking out for yourself, look out! Wesley Huber said, "There is nothing quite so dead as a self-centered man—a man who holds himself up as a self made success, and measures himself by himself and is pleased with the result." The man who believes in nothing but himself lives in a very small world. The best way to be happy is to forget yourself and focus on other people. Henry Courtney said, "The bigger a man's head gets, the easier it is to fill his shoes."

Selfishness always ends in self-destruction. Benjamin Franklin said, "A man wrapped up in himself makes a very small bundle."

Being a servant is not always the most natural thing to do. We are all conditioned to think about ourselves. That is why 97 percent of all people will write their own names when they are offered a new pen to try. Despite our tendency toward self-promotion, it is always true more is accomplished when nobody cares who gets the credit.

The old saying is true, "The way to the throne room is through the servants' quarters." One of the most powerful decisions you can make in your life is to do something for someone who does not have the power or resources to return the favor.

When you give of yourself to help other people, you cannot help but be abundantly rewarded. No one is truly a success in life until he or she has learned how to serve.

No one
is TRULY a
SUCCESS
in life until
he or she
has learned
HOW TO
SERVE.

Nº 18

Say **NO**
to many
GOOD ideas.

One of the biggest mistakes we can make is to say **yes** to too many good things. Then we end up being spread so thin we are mediocre in everything and excellent in nothing.

There is one guaranteed formula for failure, and that is to try to please everyone.

There's a big difference between something that is *good* and something that is *right*. The challenge is to distinguish the difference. Our responsibility as leaders is always to do the right things with excellence before we start diversifying into other areas.

There comes a time in every person's life when he or she must learn to **say no** to many good ideas. In fact, the more an individual grows, the more opportunities he or she will have to **say no**. One proven key to results is becoming focused. The temptation is always to do a little bit of everything.

Remember, saying *no* to a good idea does not always mean saying *never*. **"No" may mean "not right now."**

There is power in the word **no**. It breaks the yoke of over-commitment and weakness. **No** can be used to turn a situation from bad to good, from wrong to right. Saying *no* can free you from burdens you don't need to carry right now.

It also frees you to devote the correct amount of attention and effort to priorities in your life.

As you read this, **you probably recall many situations in which "no" or "not right now" would have been the right answer.** Don't put yourself through that kind of disappointment in the future.

"Yes" and "no" are the two most important words you will ever say. These are the two words that determine your destiny in life. How and when you say them affects your entire future.

Saying *no* to lesser things means saying *yes* to priorities in your life.

№ 19

There's always **FREE FOOD** on a fish **HOOK.**

Did you know the best path you can take is to do what's right, in the proper timing? Shortcuts invite compromise, strife and confusion.

We need to understand we're long-distance runners. We are not in a sprint, and we do not need to look for shortcuts that open the door to compromise.

There is an old saying that is absolutely true, "If you keep your attention on learning the tricks of the trade, you will never learn the trade." Watch out for fads—because the letters of the word stand for "for a day."

There is a story about a beautiful bird that would sit at the top of a tree and make lovely melodies. One day a man, walking through the woods, passed by the tree and heard the beautiful bird singing. The bird saw the man who was holding a box.

"What do you have in the box?" the bird asked the man.

The man replied he had large, juicy earthworms in the box. "I will sell you a worm for one of your beautiful feathers," he offered.

The bird pulled out a feather and exchanged it for a worm. He reflected to himself, *why should I work hard to get worms when it is so easy to get them this way?*

The bird and the man repeated this process over the course of many days, and soon the bird no longer had any more beautiful feathers with which to pay for worms. He could no longer fly and was no longer pretty. He did not feel like singing beautiful songs and was very unhappy.

Like this foolish bird, we are always tempted to look for shortcuts, ways to get ahead and obtain the results we desire. But as the foolish bird learned, there is a price for taking shortcuts.

Eventually we will learn there is no shortcut to success worth taking. One of the hidden truths of life is that the path to the prize is always more valuable than the prize itself. Shortcuts rob us of those valuable lessons we need to learn along the way. When you are presented with a shortcut—a way that is not right—say *no*. Be persistent and stick to the path in front of you.

Be persistent and **STICK TO THE PATH** in front of you.

Nº 20

When you **REFUSE** to change, you end up **IN CHAINS.**

Inanimate objects like clothes, houses and buildings do not have the ability to truly change. They grow out of style and become unusable. But at any point in time, at any age, any one of us is able to change.

Here's what change looks like many times. We continue to reach toward the same goal but perhaps in a slightly different way. To change does not always mean to do the opposite. In fact, most of the time, it means adding on or slightly adjusting what already exists.

The longer we take to cooperate with the change required of us, the further behind we get.

There are three things we know about the future: First, it is not going to be like the past. Second, it is not going to be exactly the way we think it will be. Third, the rate of change will take place faster than we anticipate.

In 1803, the British created a civil service position that required a man to stand on the Cliffs of Dover with a spyglass. His duty was to be a lookout against invasion. He was to ring a bell if he saw Napoleon Bonaparte's armies approaching. This job was appropriate at the time, but that job was not eliminated until 1945! How many spyglasses on the Cliffs of Dover are we still holding onto in our lives? We should not let "the way we've always done it" interfere with the opportunities in front of us today. There is nothing that remains as constant as change.

Even the most precious of all gems needs to be chiseled and faceted to achieve its best luster. So, don't end up like concrete—all mixed together and permanently set.

I believe we can decide in advance how we will respond to most situations. When I was coaching basketball many years ago, I told my players they could prepare for many situations ahead of time. We used to practice different game situations so they would know how to respond when they got into the actual situation. It worked!

Go with the flow. Be sensitive to the new things. ***Stay flexible and know you'll need to adjust, move, correct and change to be successful.***

You are *custom-built* for **CHANGE.**

Nº 21

Everything
BIG STARTS
with something
LITTLE.

All successful people are faithful in the small things. There is power in taking small steps.

Many people are not moving forward today simply because they were not willing to take the small step placed before them. If you have a dream to go into any particular area, you should leap at the opportunity—no matter how small—to move in the direction of your dream. For example: if you dream of being a college basketball coach and are sitting at home waiting for an invitation from Roy Williams at North Carolina University, you should know that call will never come. You need to find an opportunity to coach somewhere, anywhere. Find a young person, a young team. Jump in and coach with all of your heart, like you would if you were coaching at the highest level.

Don't be afraid to take small steps. There's something powerful about momentum … no matter how small. Many times the impossible is simply the untried.

I can remember a time in my life when I was immobilized with fear, consumed with what I was supposed to do. It seemed so huge a task; I was unable to bring myself to face it. A friend came to me and spoke _two words_ that broke that paralysis in my life. He said,

"Do something!" I'll never forget that day ... taking some small, seemingly insignificant steps. Momentum began to come into my life.

If you are at a point of paralysis in your life because of what you feel you're supposed to do, the words today are, "Do something!" Don't worry about the long-term goal right now; just take the steps that take you past the starting point. Soon you'll get to a point of no return. As you climb higher, you'll be able to see much farther.

As you begin, don't be afraid. Eric Hoffer said, "Fear of becoming a 'has-been' keeps some people from becoming anything." Every great idea is impossible from where you are starting today. But little goals add up, and they add up rapidly. Most people don't succeed because they are too afraid to even try. As incredible as it sounds, they decide in advance they're going to fail…

Many times the final goal seems so unreachable we don't even make an effort. But once you've made your decision and have started, it's like you're halfway there. **Start**—no matter what your circumstances. Take that first step!

It's simple. Grow wherever you're planted.

Nº 22

A chip on
the shoulder
**WEIGHS
A TON.**

Few things get you off track as fast as when someone has "done you wrong." When you decide to do anything significant with your life, you will be lied to, stolen from and taken advantage of. How you respond makes all the difference.

Who do you need to forgive? You may think of this as a spiritual or religious idea. It's also a powerful success principle.

The weight of unforgiveness greatly drags a person down. It is a tremendous load to carry in the race of life. Here's the key: If you want to travel far, travel light.

When faced with the need to forgive and forget, never make the excuse, "But you don't know what that person did to me!" That may be true, but do you know what unforgiveness will do to you?

Unforgiveness leads to great bitterness, which is a costly misuse of your creative imagination. Great amounts of brain power are used up when you ponder a negative situation and plot how to get even. This kind of thinking is totally unproductive.

What really matters is what **happens in us**, not **to** us.

Forgiveness is essential for good relationships, both person-ally and professionally. It's also a very valuable business and success principle.

People who burn bridges will find themselves isolated and alone … dealing with those who are neutral and enemies the rest of their lives. That's why we should do all we can to build bridges, not burn them. Vengeance is a poor traveling companion. Getting even always results in imbalance and unhappiness.

Working with businesses throughout America, I have found un-forgiveness in every stagnating situation. Conversely, I have found growing organizations generally don't talk that much about past problems and injustices. Successful people have a way of not let-ting things stick to them.

Never underestimate the power of forgiveness to free you to focus on your dream. It's the one power you have over a per-son who slanders or takes advantage of you. The farther you walk in forgiveness, the greater the distance you put between yourself and the negative situation. It allows you to run toward your goals and dreams unhindered.

Forgiveness is

FREEDOM.

№ 23

Your problem
is **YOUR
PROMOTION.**

Every obstacle introduces a person to himself. How we respond to our obstacles is very important.

Consider the famous story of David and Goliath. The giant Goliath, confronted and intimidated the armies of Israel, including the brothers of a young shepherd named David. David's brothers chose not to do anything about the obstacle before them, but we know David did. Why? What caused David to strike down the giant? It was what he saw. The brothers looked at the obstacle, Goliath, and figured it was *too big to hit*, but David looked at the obstacle and figured it was *too big to miss.*

The way you look at any obstacle in your life makes all the difference. Keep in mind one important fact; every obstacle has a limited life span. We all probably worried about things last year we can't even remember today. One of the biggest lies you can believe is things will not change; they will not pass.

Obstacles subdue mediocre people, but great leaders rise above them. You and I need to be like the man who, when asked what helped him overcome the obstacles of life, responded, "The other obstacles." We should be like a kite that rises against the wind, higher and higher. *Every* problem has a soft spot; there is an answer.

Many people think most of their obstacles are money-related, but the correct perspective is to know a problem that can be solved with a checkbook is not really an obstacle; it's an expense.

Henry Ford said, **"Obstacles are those frightful things you see when you take your eyes off the goal."** In times of adversity, you don't have an obstacle; you have a choice.

Let each new problem force you to go to the next level. As you do, know this: No obstacle will ever leave you the way it found you. You will be better, or you will be worse. Many times our best opportunities disguise themselves as the biggest obstacles.

OPPORTUNITIES
disguise
themselves
as the biggest
OBSTACLES.

Nº 24

"An **ARMY OF SHEEP** led by a lion would **DEFEAT** an **ARMY OF LIONS** led by a sheep."

~ *Old Arab Proverb* ~

What are the actions and attributes of leaders? What is it that makes them different from others?

1. Leaders are always full of praise.

2. Leaders learn to say "thank you" and "please" on the way to the top.

3. Leaders are always growing.

4. Leaders are possessed with dreams.

5. Leaders launch forth before success is certain.

6. Leaders are not afraid of confrontation.

7. Leaders talk about their own mistakes before they talk about someone else's.

8. Leaders are people of honesty and integrity.

9. Leaders have a good name.

10. Leaders make others better.

11. Leaders are quick to praise and encourage the smallest amount of improvement.

12. Leaders are genuinely interested in others.

13. Leaders look for and praise someone doing something right.

14. Leaders take others up with them.

15. Leaders respond to their failures before others have to reveal them.

16. Leaders never allow murmuring from themselves or others.

17. Leaders are specific about what is expected.

18. Leaders hold others accountable.

19. Leaders do what is right rather than what is popular.

20. Leaders are servants.

A leader is a lion, not a sheep.

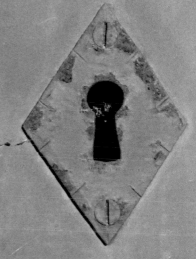

Be the
LION.
Be the
LEADER.

№ 25

People are **BORN**
ORIGINALS but
most die copies.

I come into contact with many different types of people. One time I talked on the phone with a pastor whom I had never met and who did not know me personally. We agreed I would visit his church as a consultant. As we were closing our conversation and were setting a time to meet at the local airport, he asked me, "How will I know you when you get off the plane?"

"Oh, don't worry, pastor; I'll know you," I responded jokingly. "All you pastors look alike."

The point of this humorous story is *you* must be the person *you* were made to be. If you're not you, then who are you going to be?

Average people compare themselves with others, but we should always compare ourselves with the person we believe we're supposed to be. Our standard is the unique purpose and design for our lives.

You're made a certain way. **You're unique.** To copy others is to cheat yourself of the fullness of who you are and what you can be. You and I can always find someone richer than we are, poorer than we are, or more or less able than we are. Comparison is not proof of anything.

So choose to accept and become the person you were made to be. Tap into the originality and creative genius in your life. Robert Quillen reflected, "If you count all your assets, you always show a profit."

Never judge yourself by your weaknesses. I agree with Malcolm Forbes who claimed, "Too many people overvalue what they are not and undervalue what they are." You are richer than you think you are.

Too many people take only their wants into consideration, never their talents and abilities. Deep down inside, if you are a musician, then make music. If you are a teacher, teach. Be what you are and you will be at peace with yourself.

E.E. Cummings advised, ***"To be nobody but yourself—in a world which is doing its best, night and day, to make you everybody else—means to fight the hardest battle which any human being can fight and never stop fighting."***

Do what's most natural for you. A Yoruba proverb says, "You can't stop a pig from wallowing in the mud." As Abraham Lincoln mused, "Whatever you are, be a good one."

Be Original.
Be YOU.

Nº 26

The most
UNPROFITABLE
item ever
manufactured
is an **EXCUSE.**

When it comes to excuses, the world is full of great inventors. Some spend half their lives telling what they are going to do, and the other half explaining why they didn't do it. An alibi is the proof that you did do what you didn't do, so that others will think you didn't do what you did.

You can fail many times, but you're not a failure until you begin to blame someone else. Our own mistakes fail to help us when we blame them on other people. When you use excuses, you give up your power to change.

"Never mind whom you praise, but be very careful whom you blame," said Edmund Gosse. You can fall down many times, but you won't be a failure until you say that someone else pushed you.

So, find a way, not an excuse. One who makes a mistake, and then makes an excuse for it, is making two mistakes. Note this truth: "The fox condemns the trap, not himself," said William Blake. Don't find yourself talking like that old fox!

Never complain and never explain. "Admitting error clears the score and proves you wiser than before," said Arthur Guiterman. Doing a job right is always easier than fabricating an alibi for why you didn't. The mediocre life eagerly waits to provide you with an excuse for every wrong step. Time wasted thinking up excuses and alibis would always be better spent planning, preparing and working towards your goals in life.

A real *failure* does not need an excuse.

It is an end in itself.

GERTRUDE STEIN

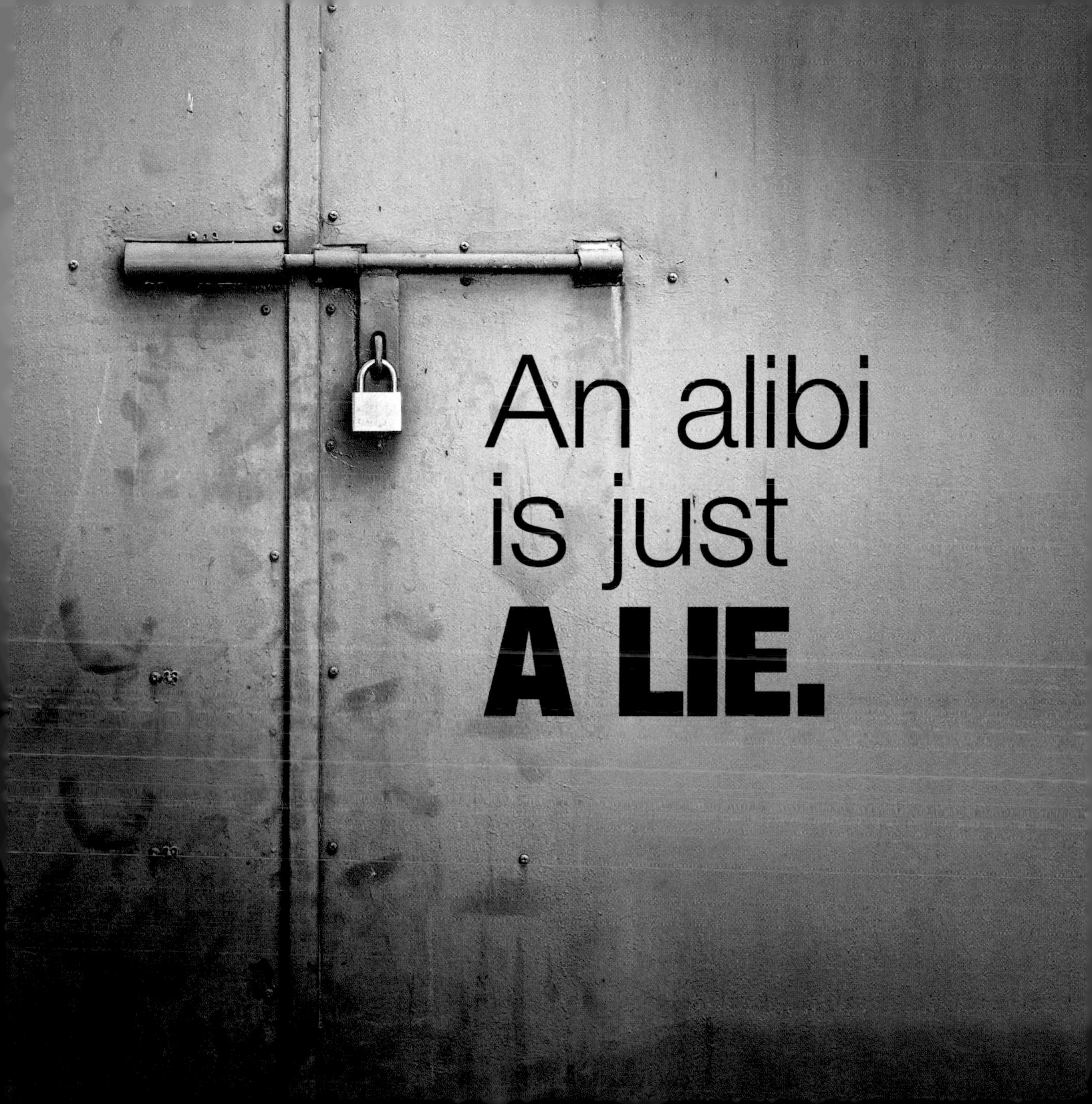
An alibi
is just
A LIE.

N⁰: 27

Don't ask time
where it's gone;
TELL IT
WHERE
TO GO!

All great achievers understand the value of maximizing their time. Each human being has been created equally in one respect. Every person has 24 hours each day. What you do with each day matters.

Give your best time to your most challenging situation. It's not how much you do that matters; it's how much you finish. Here's a key, say *no*. Not saying *no* when you should is one of the biggest causes of time wasted. This valuable saying says it all, "Don't spend a dollar's worth of time for ten cents' worth of results."

Make sure to take care of vulnerable times in your days—first thing in the morning and the last thing at night. It is amazing how much these two times influence our whole day.

If you find yourself saying, "I could be doing big things if I weren't so busy doing small things," then you need to take control of your time. The greater control you exercise over your time, the greater freedom you will experience.

I often hear people say, "I'd give anything to be able to …" If you have said this, you should adopt the "6 x 1 = 6" leadership principle. If you want to write a book, learn to play a musical instrument, become a better tennis player, or do anything else important, then you should devote one hour a day, six days a week, to the project. Your desire will become reality sooner than you think. There isn't much a person can't accomplish in 312 hours a year! A commitment of one hour a day, six days a week, is all it takes.

We all have the same amount of time each day. The difference is what we do with the amount of time at our disposal. Don't be like the airline pilot flying over the Pacific Ocean who reported to his passengers, "We're lost, but we're making great time!" Remember the future arrives an hour at a time. Gain control of your time, and you will gain control of your life.

Gain control of **YOUR TIME,** and you will gain control of **YOUR LIFE.**

Nº 28

Keep your
TEMPER.
Nobody else
wants it.

Don't fly into a rage unless you are prepared for a rough landing. Anger falls one letter short of danger. People constantly blowing fuses are generally left in the dark. If you lose your head, how can you expect to use it?

A Filipino saying advises, "Postpone today's anger until tomorrow." (Then apply this rule the next day and the next.) When you are upset, take a lesson from modern science; *always count down before blasting off.* Seneca quipped, "The best cure for anger is delay."

Blowing your stack always adds to the air pollution. You'll never get to the top if you keep blowing yours.

One of the worst fruits of anger is revenge. No passion of the human heart promises so much and pays so little as that of revenge. The longest odds in the world are those against getting even with someone. Francis Bacon adds, "In taking revenge a man is but even with his enemy; but in passing it over, he is superior."

Time spent in getting even is better used in trying to get ahead. Revenge is like biting a dog because the dog has bitten you. An Old English Proverb says, "Vengeance is a dish best eaten cold."

Marcus Antonius reflected, "Consider how much more you often suffer from your anger and grief, than from those very things for which you are angry and grieved." Anger is a boomerang that will surely hit you harder than anyone or anything at which you throw it.

> *Bitterness* is like cancer.
> It eats upon the host.
> But *anger* is like fire.
> *It burns it all clean.*
>
> MAYA ANGELOU

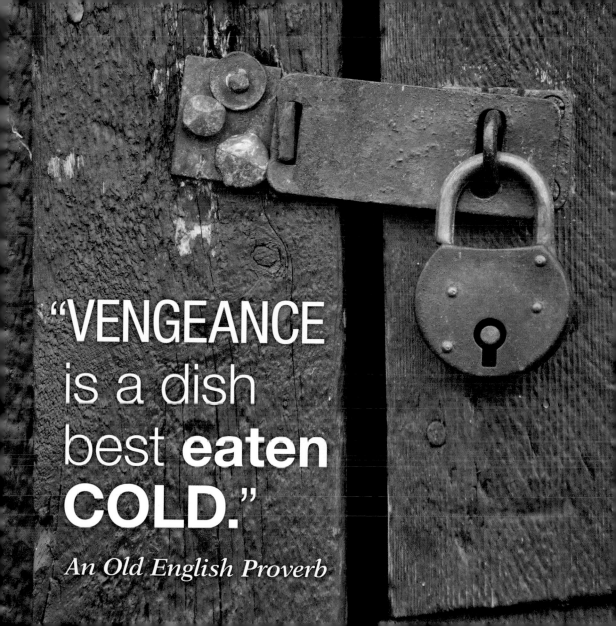

"VENGEANCE
is a dish
best **eaten**
COLD."

An Old English Proverb

N⁰ 29

Living a **DOUBLE LIFE** will get you **NOWHERE** twice as **FAST**.

Character is the real foundation of all worthwhile success. A good question to ask yourself is, "What kind of world would this world be if everybody were just like me?" You are simply a book telling the world about its author. John Morely remarked, "No man can climb out beyond the limitations of his own character."

Never be ashamed of doing right. Marcus Aurelius exhorted, "Never esteem anything as of advantage to thee that shall make thee break thy word or lose thy self-respect."

You do not need to say, "I will be bad." You only have to say, "I will not choose the best choice," and the evidence of a damaged reputation is already settled. There is no such thing as a *necessary evil.* Phillips Brooks said, "A man who *lives* right and is right has more power in his silence than another has by his words."

Many a man's reputation would not recognize his character if they met in the dark. To change your character, you must begin at the control center—the heart. Personal bankruptcy is inevitable when a man is no longer able to keep the interest paid on his moral obligations.

Henry Ward Beecher said, ***"No man can tell whether he is rich or poor by turning to his ledger. It is the heart that makes a***

man rich. He is rich according to what he is, not according to what he has.” Live so that your friends can defend you, but never have to do so. Consider what Woodrow Wilson said, “If you will think about what you ought to do for other people, your character will take care of itself.” Excellence in character is shown by doing unwitnessed what we would be doing with the whole world watching.

Let me pose this question for you: *Would the boy/girl you were be proud of the man/woman you are?* You're called to grow like a tree, not like a mushroom. It's hard to climb high when your character is low. The world's shortest and best speech is said by the traffic sign: *Keep Right.*

A FINAL **Word**

Be the whole person you can be. Don't settle for anything less. Don't look back. Look forward and decide today to boldly take steps toward the very best plans for your life.

About the **AUTHOR**

John Mason is a national best-selling author, noted speaker and executive author coach. He is the founder and president of Insight International, an organization dedicated to helping people reach their dreams and fulfill their destinies.

He has authored 14 books including *An Enemy Called Average, You're Born An Original-Don't Die A Copy,* and *Know Your Limits—Then Ignore Them* which have sold over 1.4 million copies and been translated into 30 languages throughout the world. These books are widely known as a source of sound wisdom, genuine motivation and practical principles. His writings have been published in *Reader's Digest,* along with numerous other national and international publications.

Known for his quick wit, powerful thoughts and insightful ideas, he's a popular speaker across the U.S. and around the world.

John and his wife, Linda, have four children: Michelle, Greg, Michael and David. They reside in Tulsa, Oklahoma.

John Mason welcomes the opportunity to speak for your business or organization. He's a very popular communicator on a variety of topics, including leadership, motivation and success.

John Mason
www.freshword.com
contact@freshword.com
Insight International
P.O. Box 54996
Tulsa, OK 74155

If you have enjoyed this book, we invite you to check out our entire collection of gift books with free inspirational movies, at **www.simpletruths.com.** You'll discover it's a great way to inspire friends and family, or to thank your best customers and employees.

For more information, please visit us at:

www.simpletruths.com

or call us toll free …

800-900-3427